HAL•LEONARD
INSTRUMENTAL
PLAY-ALONG

AUDIO
ACCESS
INCLUDED

PLAYBACK+
Speed • Pitch • Balance • Loop

FLUTE

Disney FROZEN

T0082038

Audio arrangements by Peter Deneff

To access audio visit:
www.halleonard.com/mylibrary

Enter Code
4822-3734-2059-3366

Disney Characters and Artwork © 2019 Disney

ISBN 978-1-5400-8374-6

Visit Hal Leonard Online at
www.halleonard.com

Contact us:
Hal Leonard
7777 West Bluemound Road
Milwaukee, WI 53213
Email: info@halleonard.com

In Europe, contact:
Hal Leonard Europe Limited
42 Wigmore Street
Marylebone, London, W1U 2RN
Email: info@halleonardeurope.com

In Australia, contact:
Hal Leonard Australia Pty. Ltd.
4 Lentara Court
Cheltenham, Victoria, 3192 Australia
Email: info@halleonard.com.au

ALL IS FOUND

FLUTE

Music and Lyrics by KRISTEN ANDERSON-LOPEZ
and ROBERT LOPEZ

SOME THINGS NEVER CHANGE

Flute

Music and Lyrics by KRISTEN ANDERSON-LOPEZ
and ROBERT LOPEZ

INTO THE UNKNOWN

Flute

Music and Lyrics by KRISTEN ANDERSON-LOPEZ
and ROBERT LOPEZ

LOST IN THE WOODS

Flute

Music and Lyrics by KRISTEN ANDERSON-LOPEZ
and ROBERT LOPEZ

THE NEXT RIGHT THING

FLUTE

Music and Lyrics by KRISTEN ANDERSON-LOPEZ
and ROBERT LOPEZ

REINDEER(S) ARE BETTER THAN PEOPLE (CONT.)

FLUTE

Music and Lyrics by KRISTEN ANDERSON-LOPEZ
and ROBERT LOPEZ

SHOW YOURSELF

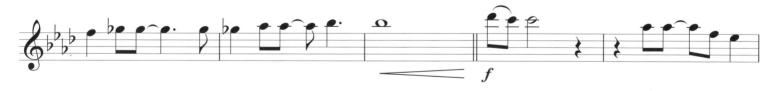

WHEN I AM OLDER

Flute

Music and Lyrics by KRISTEN ANDERSON-LOPEZ
and ROBERT LOPEZ